Clever Rabbit
and the Wolves

Retold by
Susanna Davidson

Illustrated by
Emilie Vanvolsem

Reading consultant: Alison Kelly
Roehampton University

Clever Rabbit
was trapped.

He was in the middle
of a ring of wolves.

"Mmm! Dinner!"
said Big Wolf.

"Wait!" said Clever Rabbit.

"Don't you want to see my dance?"

"No!" said Big Wolf.

5

"I want to see your dance," said Little Wolf.

Clever Rabbit tapped
his foot.

He sang.

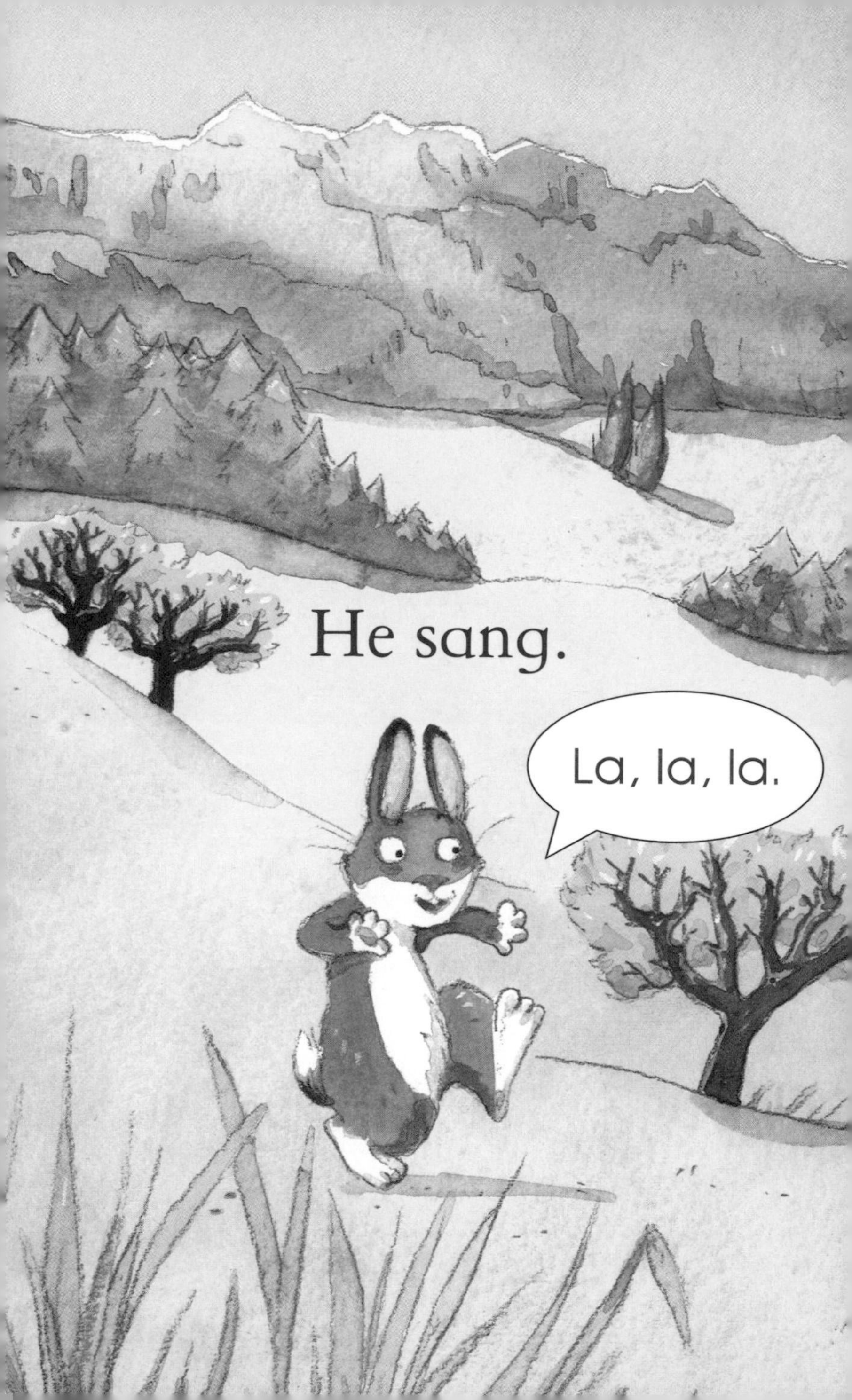

"Stomp your foot on the word la. Copy me."

All the wolves stomped
their feet.

"This is fun," they said.

"Show us more!"

13

sang Clever Rabbit.

"Turn around on the
word tum."

"This is easy," said
Big Wolf.

"Oh yes?" said Clever
Rabbit.

"Try it faster."

La-la-la! Tum-tum-tum!

sang Clever Rabbit.

He sang it faster
and faster.

The wolves stomped
their feet.

They turned around
and around.

"I'm dizzy," said Little Wolf.

Clever Rabbit danced
into the long grass.

"Keep dancing," he called.

La-la-la! Tum-tum-tum!
La-la-la! Tum-tum-tum!

One by one, the wolves
fell to the ground.

"Where's that rabbit?"
asked Big Wolf.

But Clever Rabbit was far away...

...and the wolves were too dizzy to chase him.

PUZZLES

Puzzle 1

Can you spot the differences between these two pictures?

There are six to find.

Puzzle 2
Put the pictures in order.

a   b   c   d

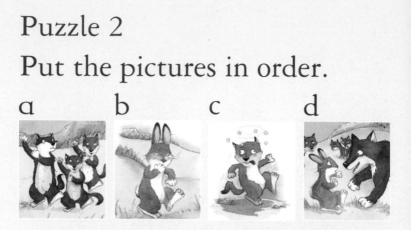

Puzzle 3
What happened next?

a

or

b

Puzzle 4
Choose the best sentence in each picture.

Answers to puzzles

Puzzle 1

Puzzle 2

d   b   a   c

Puzzle 3

a

Puzzle 4

I'm dizzy.   I'm dancing.

Designed by Caroline Spatz
Series designer: Russell Punter
Series editor: Lesley Sims
Digital manipulation: Nick Wakeford

First published in 2008 by Usborne Publishing Ltd., Usborne House,
83-85 Saffron Hill, London EC1N 8RT, England. www.usborne.com
Copyright © 2008 Usborne Publishing Ltd.